Good Grief

Where's Daddy?

By Raynisha Chester

Copyright © 2021 by Raynisha Chester

All rights reserved. No part of this book may be reproduced or used in any manner without written permission of the copyright owners except for the use of quotations in a book review or for educational purposes.

Before reading this book to your child, I highly suggest that you perform the exercise listed below.

Give the child a few balloons to play with. Some loose, some tied to a string, or one on their bed post. The objective is to give them enough time for nature to run its course allowing for a teachable moment.

In addition, if you have not already had a balloon releasing ceremony, you and your child can perform one of your own. Try places like your backyard, a park or the beach. This is so that the child can fully see the story come to life.

Lastly, this book does make mention of the word "died." If you are not comfortable with the verbiage on page 11, you can substitute it.

Ex: Remember when your balloon popped and you were sad? Just like that balloon, daddy has passed.

Thank you for your support!

It stayed with you all day and all night.

Just like that balloon sadly, daddy has died.

Remember when everyone came to say goodbye?

Beyond the sky is where heaven is, that is where daddy now lives.

But when you miss his face and his voice,

you can watch him in a video of your choice.

Daddy loves you and he will always be in your heart. Put your hand over your chest... feel that? That is the best part.